Credit Score Hacks

How to Boost Your Credit Score Fast
and Keep it Great

Scribe

Scribe

Scribe
New York / Wyoming

This Scribe trade paperback edition September 2017

For information about special discounts for bulk purchases, please contact Scribe at hello@thescri.be.

Cover art designed by Francisco Reynoso.

ISBN-10:0-9974112-0-1
ISBN-13:978-0-9974112-0-1

See Scribe books at: www.shindychen.com/scribe.

Contents

Preface

We're in a new age of credit.

Back in 2014, I wrote "The Credit Cleanup Book."

It was the first book to address how consumers could understand, repair, and maintain their credit scores after 2008's financial crisis and economic turmoil.

I wrote it based on my years of lending experience, first as loan originator and later as a V.P. in lending at one of the nation's largest banks, where I worked with hundreds of consumer credit profiles.

Now, three years later, I present: "Credit Score Hacks: How to Boost Your Credit Score Fast and Keep it Great."

The Fundamentals of the First Book are Here

I've included the need-to-know fundamentals from the first book, such as getting your credit report, learning how to read it, and understanding how it's scored. I also revisit the long-term behaviors that will help maintain a healthy credit rating.

You can call this part, "The Credit Cleanup Book, Lite."

What's New

In *Credit Score Hacks*, I list ways to improve your credit score by targeting each of the 5 factors of credit scoring.

Even if you can't target them all at once, you can execute on tactics that combine to improve your credit rating, make it great, and keep it there—all while avoiding costly credit repair services and unnecessary debt management solutions.

Once you get that great credit score, you'll be able to use it to apply for really high-end premium cards with excellent sign-up bonuses, and get the lowest possible rate for other loans.

In this book I also discuss new credit rules that can benefit every day consumers, such as more leniency when it comes to medical debts, and greater accuracy required of any civil debts and judgments appearing on consumer credit files.

Today, the Consumer Financial Protection Bureau (CFPB) is the government watchdog of credit reporting agencies (CRAs), banks, lenders, and other financial companies.

There are new mobile and web app technologies that allow consumers to get their credit scores right away. It's easier than ever to know where you stand when it comes to your credit rating.

These same technologies can analyze your spending behaviors and tell you how to manage your finances better. They say they can tell you how to boost your score, instead of you trying to do it all yourself.

But with new technologies come additional security risks that must be managed properly. As the major Equifax data breach in September 2017 shows, no company is safe from attack; I'll help you understand how you can use credit and identity-theft monitoring to keep an eye on your credit data.

Master Credit Basics and Learn Quick Score Boosting Hacks

Despite all of these credit industry trends, the tenets of what make a good credit score haven't changed.

If you pay your bills on time, keep your credit cards from being maxed out, mix up your loans with credit cards, and don't apply for too much new credit in too short of a timeframe, then you're on the right track.

But this is easier said than done, and many consumers still find mastering the basics a mystery.

They also don't know about the quick hacks that can really boost your score, and that is where my tips will help.

So, without any further ado, let's get started. Well done for picking up this book and taking the first step toward mastering your greatest financial asset: your credit score.

Sincerely,
Shindy Chen, Author

P.S. If you'd like to stay in touch with me and get regular, valuable credit news you can actually use, sign up for The Credit Cleanup Newsletter at tccbonline.com/newsletter.

CHAPTER 1:
3 Credit Bureaus, 3 Credit Scores, Endless Financial Data

The history of credit reporting and scoring isn't so boring—honest.

It's actually the story about how we lost our privacy to companies who are now gathering, reporting, and selling information about us.

This data is valuable to advertisers, and reveals our financial and spending behaviors.

When you ask to borrow money for a car or house, to get a new credit card, or to start basic utility services such as new home internet or cell phone service, your credit data is used to judge how well you can pay on-time for these loans and services.

A Mini-History of Credit Reporting

Back in the day, when people purchased on credit, banks would keep internal ledgers on their clients' individual payment histories, and then exchange this information with other banks.

Imagine how the administrative paperwork looked, *way* before Excel spreadsheets, Google Sheets, and even smartphone apps that now know everything about how you save, spend, and pay your bills.

Soon, companies that managed these records cropped up, and as technology improved so did the abilities to organize more information, automate it, and make faster credit decisions.

Equifax

The first CRA was the Retail Credit Company, which eventually became Equifax in 1999.

Born in Atlanta, Georgia in 1899—where it is still headquartered today—Equifax started as a business-to-business data provider for life, auto, medical, and insurance policy applicants.

Today, Equifax sells information, software, analytics, and consumer and business credit reports, primarily to insurance and health care providers, utilities companies, government agencies, and financial institutions. Other products offered include credit fraud and identity protection monitoring services.

TransUnion

TransUnion was created in 1968 and has evolved over the years in its business-to-business products.

In its early days, TransUnion was actually at the forefront of technology, enabling tape-to-disc transfer of consumer data, as well as creating the first online information storage and retrieval data processing system, which drastically sped up lending decisions.

Today, TransUnion's consumer business, started in 2002, offers credit products including credit reports.

Experian

Technically the youngest of three bureaus by name only, Experian is a result of over a hundred years of mergers among both U.K. and U.S. data and retail companies.

Since then, Experian has listed itself as a public company on the London Stock Exchange, and continues on its path to global information domination, even recently acquiring Brazil's largest credit bureau, Serasa, in 2007.

Credit Scoring Is Born

In 1956, an engineer named Bill Fair and a mathematician named Earl Isaac founded Fair Isaac and Company, better known today as FICO.

The pair worked to convince lenders that their mathematical formulas generated more reliable data from consumer credit histories.

Until then, credit reports weren't always numbers-based, and contained abstract (even discriminatory) information about a person's sexual orientation, drinking habits, and cleanliness, which was culled from questionable or even fake news sources.

People suspected that their credit reports were being used against them, and felt left in in the dark about what was in their personal files.

FICO aimed to change that. With their credit-scoring algorithms, the formulas would look past a person's age, race, or identifying information.

With FICO data, an applicant's creditworthiness could be predicted faster than any error-prone manual human methods.

Gone were the biases the decision makers were using as qualifying metrics at the time.

With FICO's formulas and superfast computer processing, today's billion-dollar credit industry was born.

FICO Scores + Credit Reporting

All three credit bureaus incorporate FICO's formulas into their credit scoring models.

There's a misnomer that a "FICO score" represents or is tied to a *single* credit bureau.

In fact, all three credit bureaus use some version of FICO's data modeling within their credit scoring methods, but they differ in the weights assigned to certain criteria over others.

Which is why, if you've pulled your credit report previously, you get three *similar, but not identical*, scores. (How credit is scored is further discussed in Chapter 4, "How Credit is Scored.")

To add confusion to the process, each bureau's FICO scores have taken on nicknames of their own.

Effective marketing by the CRAs and lending industries have now created so many different credit score types that it's easy to lose track of what's what.

FICO Score Names and Ranges

Below are each credit reporting CRAs' own FICO score names and scoring ranges:

CRA	FICO Score Name	Score Range
Equifax	Beacon	300–850
Experian	PLUS	330–830
Transunion	Empirica	400–925

If you've recently applied for a loan and the loan representative said, "Your 'Beacon' score is 745," then it means that the lender consulted Equifax for a credit report and score.

The *Beacon* score is simply Equifax's FICO score for its consumer unit.

Three Sides to the Story

One report does not a whole financial picture make. Regardless, service providers and lenders often base their lending decisions off of one credit bureau's report.

It's the equivalent of judging a news story, lovers quarrel, or any other situation by only one source. It may sound unfair, but as the stakes get higher, the more thorough lenders are likely to be.

For example, when I applied for auto loan financing, only single credit reports were pulled on both occasions. When I applied to borrow way more money for the mortgages on my houses, the lenders definitely checked my credit reports from all three bureaus.

Where one report may not suffice, the lender will want the full background on the loan candidate, which is wise considering that data may vary depending on factors as simple as the candidate's geographical location, bureau to bureau.

Single versus tri-merge reports are explained further in Chapter 2, "How to Get Credit Reports and Scores."

But Wait, There's One More

To spur up competition against FICO, the three CRAs actually collaborated to create the VantageScore model in 2006. They touted this score to be a more innovative and consistent approach to scoring.

VantageScore's methodology mirrors FICO's model, but goes further in assigning a letter grade and a numerical grade.

But, VantageScore hasn't quite pushed FICO off its throne. The FICO score remains the most popular model in use by lenders. In a 2012 CFPB report, FICO scores accounted for over 90 percent of the market of scores sold to firms in 2010 for use in credit-related decisions.

Wall Street also continues to put its faith in the quality of mortgages based on the FICO scores that were used to underwrite and qualify those mortgages.

One Group to Rule All

Since its inception in 2011, the Consumer Financial Protection Bureau, or CFPB, has penalized companies and people for violating federal consumer financial protection laws. As of this writing, it had successfully sought over 11.9 billion in relief for illegal practices.

According to a July 2013 bulletin, its main purpose continues to be to hold companies accountable when it comes to "unfair, deceptive, or abusive acts or practices in the collection of consumer debts."

Consumers can submit complaints against companies for investigation directly on the CFPB's website. If the bureau finds evidence of practices that can harm consumers, it takes actions to protect them.

It has the authority to issue penalties for violations of a range of laws, but the majority of fines issued to date have been for violations of several specific statutes, most often the Dodd-Frank Wall Street Reform and Consumer Protection Act of 2010.

In 2014 alone, the bureau issued more than $3 billion in fines, with more than $2 billion of those penalties from a case concerning mortgage servicing violations against Ocwen Financial Corp. and Ocwen Loan Servicing, LLC. Other big CFPB targets have been financial institutions such as Bank of America, Synchrony Bank, and JPMorgan Chase.

CHAPTER 2:
How to Get Credit Reports and Scores

You're now going to learn how to get your credit report and scores.

We know there are a gazillion providers, but which are best?

For example, some provide free reports; yet they don't offer credit scores. And some providers offer scores without the details of your credit lines and payment histories.

Today, more and more companies offer simple scores for free, but no insights or guidance on how to improve them.

Some companies may also require add-on monthly credit monitoring subscriptions before revealing your scores.

And finally, the most important question: Which scores or reports matter most?

The Difference Between Single and Tri-Merge Credit Reports

When lenders and service providers such as utilities providers prequalify you for loans and services, they may only pull a credit report from a single credit bureau, such as Equifax, or Experian, or TransUnion, but not all three together.

This allows them to get a quick picture of a loan candidate, and single reports are cheaper than full tri-merge reports.

A single report, however, may not tell the loan candidate's full credit story.

A tri-merge report is more detailed and reconciles all three major CRAs' data into one file. Rather than consult three separate files, the data is merged in one report for reference.

Many times, a *negative* credit item reported by one bureau may actually show to be in *good* standing by the other two credit bureaus. And while the account might very well be in good standing, if a lender makes a decision based on a single CRA report that contains negative information, it is unlikely to offer the best outcome in terms of product, service or rate. The onus is always on the consumer to contact the credit bureau responsible, and demand for the negative item to be updated or removed from its records.

Location, Location, Location

One practical reason for credit reporting inaccuracies by the CRA may simply be due to each bureau's geographical location in relation to the report holder.

For instance Equifax is based in Atlanta, Georgia, whereas TransUnion is headquartered in Chicago, Illinois. A person living in the southeastern United States may simply have more information on the Equifax report than in the TransUnion report.

Perhaps a judgment or lien filed in local courts shows on the person's Equifax report but is missing from the TransUnion report because of the processing time required for this data to reach TransUnion's records.

Or perhaps a recently paid collection to a local property management company only shows on Equifax's report, but is still showing as unpaid on the TransUnion report, again, simply due to geography and timing.

Your Options: Free and Paid Credit Reports, Free Credit Scores

With all the options out there, keep in mind that the more thorough credit information you want, the more you're going to pay.

You want to figure out whether you're more concerned about convenience, cost, or the level of detail you want about your credit data.

Option 1: Free Annual Credit Reports from the CRAs

The major CRAs offer you one free credit report every year as required under the Fair Credit Reporting Act (FCRA), and specifically the Fair and Accurate Credit Transactions Act (FACTA).

Remember that these free reports only disclose credit history and not scores.

Nonetheless, it's an economical way to see what each CRA has on file for you and to check consistency across reports.

You can order your reports easily and online with one form at www.annualcreditreport.com.

Once you order your reports, paper versions usually arrive within 15 days. You will receive separate reports, one from each CRA.

You may think, "Why would I request anything by snail mail when I can get it instantaneously online?"

It's true that we live in an on-demand digital age, but remember that when ordering or buying anything online, you become subject to any seller's or provider's terms and conditions, arbitration agreements, and limitations on liability.

I'm not saying to not order the reports online, but I just want you to be aware of what you're agreeing to before you get your reports.

I repeat this later, in Chapter 5 , where I discuss the process of disputing inaccurate credit items. If you end up having to dispute or request any removal of negative and inaccurate information, it's recommended to *do it in writing and not online.* Personally, I have always requested credit reports and made disputes in writing.

Option 2: Paid Tri-Merge Reports *with Scores,* from Credit Reporting Agencies

Getting your free reports at www.annualcreditreport.com is a great way to check on the accuracy of your personal credit history on file with the majors.

But getting your full credit reports with scores will usually require some money. You may find that you'll need to know your credit score if you're applying for a loan for major purchase such as a car or house.

> "For some reason, the geniuses of credit reporting decided it'd be a good idea to offer the physical report for free once a year and dangle the actual score itself in front of us like a juicy carrot. If you want to find out your actual credit *score* you usually have to pay and endure a barrage of ads for all sorts of different credit monitoring products in the meantime."
>
> — Business Insider

Instead of buying separate scored reports, there are options for you to purchase all three CRA reports with scores merged into one, also known as a tri-merge report.

This consolidates the paperwork into one document. While it may be convenient to seek out this one-stop shop credit report with the trifecta of data you seek, just remember that the CRAs don't offer it for free, and sometimes not cheaply, either.

There are costs involved in obtaining this data—it just depends on your personal preference for convenience over cost. At the time of writing, Equifax and Experian offered tri-merge reports at around $40, while TransUnion did not offer a tri-merge report.

The direct-from-CRA reports are going to give you the Beacon, FICO, and Empirica scores you often hear about.

> **PRO-TIP**: If you're currently in the process of getting a preapproval for a mortgage or car loan, ask your loan officer or loan representative for a copy of your credit report.
>
> What's the worst that could happen? They say no. Your loan representative probably won't have a problem with it unless the company prevents the person from doing so.
>
> As a loan officer, I was happy to include a copy of my clients' credit reports along with their loan application.

Equifax

Equifax offers a single consolidated tri-merge report with scores and data from all three CRAs, merged into one, for about $40.

Link: www.equifax.com/credit-bureau-report

Experian

Experian also offers a tri-merge report at the same cost ($40) as Equifax's tri-merge report.

Link: www.experian.com/consumer-products/credit-score.html

The statistics aren't available regarding how many orders the CRAs get for their products.

Part of the reason why most people don't care to order their personal credit reports directly from the CRAs is to avoid subscriptions of add-on products they don't need, such as credit monitoring or more frequent credit scores and reports.

I hate entering my credit card information for anything that's promised as free or even as low as $1 and then *having to remind myself* to go back and cancel any service or subscription.

This kind of marketing tactic loops customers in, in hopes that they will forget about or avoid the hassle to cancel said services. It's such a successful tactic that it racks up roughly $6 billion in American cardholder revenues every year.

Remember that CRAs are also in the business to collect and report consumer data, so they sell consumer products and monitoring as additional revenue streams.

Option 3: Paid Tri-Merge Reports *with Scores*, from Third-Parties

Aside from buying tri-merge reports directly from the CRAs, you can also purchase them from non-CRA sources.

MyFico.com

MyFico.com is the consumer arm of FICO and provides your FICO scores along with credit reports from the three CRAs in a side-by-side comparison. However, you'll have to cough up around $60, which is more expensive than the reports from Equifax and Experian.

MyFico.com also offers a credit simulator tool, which shows how certain activities, such as paying down debt or opening new credit, can impact credit scores.

Since then, similar tools have emerged and are wildly popular with consumers. These free tools demystify the weights and balances of how credit is scored.

Option 4: Free Scores from Third-Parties

Now that we've seen paid tri-merge report options, let's discover free ways to obtain your scores.

Luckily, there are plenty of innovative services and financial companies that provide your valuable score data for free. Keep in mind that these scores vary depending on which CRA's data is used.

In addition to getting your score, these services have also evolved since *The Credit Cleanup Book* was published in 2014. They are smarter, more robust, and offer way more features per service, so you could essentially use just one service for all of your budgeting, saving, and credit monitoring activities.

Here are the most popular methods.

Credit Sesame

A consumer favorite, Credit Sesame is both a mobile app and web-based service that lets you get your Experian score, totally free, without requiring any credit card information, and without subscribing to any services.

It also has a free credit monitoring service that alerts you of any changes or new activity to your credit report. Additional paid services include identity-theft monitoring with add-on social security number (SSN) geolocator features, which will alert you wherever your SSN is used for new credit applications.

The company launched at TechCrunch Disrupt in 2010. As of this writing, Credit Sesame analyzes roughly $35 billion in registered users' loans on a daily basis for potential consumer savings.

In addition to getting your free Experian score, the service recommends loans and credit offers that may be a good fit for you, based on your credit score and history.

When I spoke with the former CMO, Olivier Lemaignen, he said, "You'll eventually get offered rates that are similar to what our system recommended in the first place, because we've done the pre-screening and analyzing beforehand for you."

Credit Sesame also has a breadth of consumer-focused content on its blog. "We invest a lot of time writing original content to put education at the forefront. We are the most interviewed, quoted, Reddit-ed, wide-variety, not product-based, unbiased education center for consumers," Lemaignen said.

Credit Karma

Credit Karma was founded in 2007 and provides a score based on TransUnion data. It also does this for free with no credit card and no hidden costs or obligations.

It also provides account and transactions monitoring (if you link your bank and credit accounts), savings recommendations, consumer reviews, and advice from its more than 30 million other members.

Credit Karma also has a highly rated app for iPhone and Android, and you can check your credit score and receive credit monitoring alerts from the app, anywhere.

According to Credit Karma, their distinct goal is to always offer their services and educational resources for free to consumers. There are no trial subscriptions and no premium access accounts.

Clarity Money

There's a new app and web-based service which claims to be the "Mint on Steroids," called Clarity Money.

After launching in January 2017, it already has over 500,000 users and does all of what Credit Karma and Credit Sesame can do (budgeting tools, spending tracking and analysis, synced accounts, free credit scores and alerts).

But Clarity Money goes a step further by offering users the chance to create a savings account within the service and automatically save toward goals. (Full disclosure: I also advise and have written for Clarity Money in an editorial capacity.)

Clarity Money displays a user's TransUnion score, and also sends regular alerts if your score goes up or down and reasons that might have caused the change.

I'm a user too, and I must say that it is the new robust kid on the block when it comes to being an all-in-one financial app.

Also, it was recommended by Prosper Daily (RIP), formerly my favorite budgeting and expense-tracking app.

How Do They Make Money?

Ever wonder how the companies offering free scores actually make money?

While the upside is that you get your credit scores for free, the downside is that *you* are the product.

Advertisers pay these services to get access to users, data, and hundreds of thousands of potential new customers.

Once you submit your information and your credit score and history are logged, the promotional offers begin.

Advertisers don't actually see any personal user data, but they can rely on the services to pre-screen the best applicants based on user data—it's still up to individual users to submit their own information via a separate application.

When you apply for an offer and get approved, then the advertiser pays a referral fee to the service provider (Credit Karma, Credit Sesame, and Clarity Money).

Of course, promotional credit offers aren't all bad; you might very well find a better offer on a credit card or loan.

Ultimately, free credit score services are reverse lead-generation tools for creditors. And the creditors do the heavy lifting of prescreening the best customers for their products.

Aside from that, they do offer a great service for consumers who simply want to get a free credit score and know where they stand credit-wise.

CHAPTER 3:
How to Read Your Credit Report

Let's decipher a credit report.

Each section is relevant and serves its own unique purpose and my goal is to make this as painless as possible.

What's a Credit Report?

A credit report is a record of the entire history of your debts.

It is also a snapshot of your balances owed on any lines of credit or debt you have at this very moment.

Any time you provide your social security number (SSN) to borrow money or open a credit line, this activity is recorded on your credit report.

Likewise, as you pay down a loan or credit card, this activity is also recorded on your credit report.

If you have any negative credit items, such as collections, liens, bankruptcies, and foreclosures, these are included on your credit report.

Finally, credit reports also include recent credit inquiries, as well as name and address verification information.

Introducing: Barry Borrower

Take a look at the sample credit report on the next pages.

It's a report for our friend Barry Borrower.

Remember that all documents referenced throughout this book are also available at www. tccbonline.com.

No matter from where you obtain your credit report, you're sure to see the same sections of information.

You'll notice that Barry's report is an example of a "tri-merge" report, which includes all three CRA reports merged in one file.

Courtesy of The Credit Cleanup Book

Sample Basic Credit Report

Personal Information

Barry Borrower
300 Perry Street
New York, New York 10014

SSN: 234-56-7890

Company Details

Report ID:
5557678
Report Date: 10/2014

Any information input to obtain the report, including: Name, Address and SSN appears at the top. The credit reporting company's reference information will be here as well. Be sure your personal information is accurately reflected.

Credit Scores

680
TransUnion / FICO

705
Experian / Fair Isaac

725
Equifax / Beacon

A credit score, or credit scores per credit bureau, appear prominently.

General Information / Alerts

NAME MISMATCH: 1/2013
ADDRESS MISMATCH: 10/2006

ID, address mismatch alerts and consumer statements are noted.

Potentially Negative Items

Proportion of revolving balances is too high
Previous collection or charge-off

General notes about potentially negative items may appear here. Note that these may be broad in scope and based on previous credit behaviors not the most credit activity.

Credit and Trade Lines

Creditor:
Lexus Financial

Date Opened:	Balance:	High Limit:	Last Reported:	Type:	Terms:
5/13	$15,402	$29,000	10/14	Installment	36

Monthly Payment: $870 | **Status:** On Time | **Derogatory:**

Creditor:
Discover

Date Opened:	Balance:	High Limit:	Last Reported:	Type:	Terms:
3/12	$5,250	$9,000	10/14	Revolving	

Monthly Payment: $325 | **Status:** On Time | **Derogatory:**

Trade and credit lines will appear with full payment histories, minimum monthly payment requirements, status, account details, original open date, terms, and other information. Closed or paid-in-full accounts will also appear here.

Shindy Chen

Credit and Trade Lines

Creditor:
Chase

Date Opened:	Balance:	High Limit:	Last Reported:	Type:	Terms:
4/10	$750	$4,500	9/14	Revolving	

Monthly Payment:		Status:	Derogatory:		
$25		On Time			

Creditor:
Bank of America Visa

Date Opened:	Balance:	High Limit:	Last Reported:	Type:	Terms:
2/08	$2,500	$8,325	10/14	Revolving	

Monthly Payment:		Status:	Derogatory:		
$175		On Time	30 Days, 6/10		

Creditor:
Sallie Mae

Date Opened:	Balance:	High Limit:	Last Reported:	Type:	Terms:
3/06	$39,934	$75,000	10/14	Installment	15

Monthly Payment:		Status:	Derogatory:		
$634		On Time			

Creditor:
MasterCard

Date Opened:	Balance:	High Limit:	Last Reported:	Type:	Terms:
1/06	$4,500	$6,000	10/14	Revolving	

Monthly Payment:		Status:	Derogatory:		
$175		On Time			

CLOSED

Creditor:
Bank of America Visa

Date Opened:	Balance:	High Limit:	Last Reported:	Type:	Terms:
5/06	$189,124	$215,000	12/13	Installment	360

Monthly Payment:		Status:	Derogatory:		
$1,255		PAID IN FULL			

Derogatory Information

COLLECTION:
Con Edison

Date Opened: **Balance:** **Last Reported:**
1/10 $262 2/10

Monthly Payment: **Status:**
$25 PAID IN FULL

Public Records, Collections, Charge-offs, Bankruptcies, Foreclosures and any other derogatory information are listed in this section, along with the respective status.

Inquiries

Capital One 3/2014
Best Rate Mortgage Company 1/2014
Best Buy 1/2013
Verizon Wireless 10/2012

A list of the most recent requests for your credit history. Some reports may provide a more thorough list that separates inquires initiated by you, or by creditors who are screening to make credit offers.

Personal Statements

CONSUMER STATEMENT: PLEASE CONTACT ME AT 212-555-5555 FOR ANY NEW CREDIT ACCOUNT REQUESTS.

Any personal statements provided to creditors to prevent consumer fraud, or any explanation on facts or conditions of any items on the credit report.

Personal History and Verification Data

Borrower, Barry
AKA
Borrowerz, Barry SSN: 234-56-7890
NAME MISMATCH
1/2013

Borrower, Barry
AKA
Borrower, Baron SSN: 234-56-7890
NAME MISMATCH
10/2012

Current Address:
300 Perry Street
New York, NY 10014
Reported 10/2012

Previous Address: **Previous Address:** **Previous Address:**
100 Fulton Street 250 Desbrosses Street 120 Peachtree Road
New York, NY 10038 New York, NY 10013 Atlanta, GA 30324
Reported 8/2009 Reported 10/2006 Reported 10/2006

Any addresses, aliases and dates of birth reported by data providers, to further verify consumer information. Name, address or SSN mismatches may also be noted in this section.

Now, let's go through each section of Barry's credit report.

The Sample Credit Report

Personal Information

At the top of any credit report is the information that was provided to obtain it.

Your full legal name, current address, and SSN (or a truncated version of your SSN) will appear in this section and it should be accurate.

Depending on the company or CRA used to generate the report, a tracking number for your report may also show here, much like it does on Barry's report

Credit Scores

For credit reports with scores, you'll see your three-digit credit score(s) for each credit bureau prominently located near the top (more details on credit scoring are discussed in Chapter 4).

For Barry's tri-merge report, looks like his three scores from the major CRAs are 680, 705, and 725.

General Information and Alerts

This section flags any name or address mismatches, fraud alerts, and consumer statements tied to a personal credit report.

Name and Address Mismatches

We can see that Barry's report includes a name mismatch logged in January 2013 and an address mismatch in October 2006. Lenders may wish to verify this data with Barry during a loan application, just to confirm his identifying information.

General Information / Alerts		ID, address mismatch alerts and consumer statements are noted.
NAME MISMATCH:	1/2013	
ADDRESS MISMATCH:	10/2006	

Don't be alarmed if you see a name or address mismatch alert on your personal report, as this occurs quite frequently.

A *name mismatch* is quite common. Whenever the identifying information used to pull a credit report is different from the data within the report itself, it is logged within the credit reporting data and history.

For example, if a person's legal first name is *James* and a lender has pulled a credit report on James's behalf using his nickname *Jim*, then a name mismatch is triggered as simple as that.

This also happens when a person goes by a middle name, for which a lender may input as the first name for credit report–pulling purposes, unaware of the name variation.

An example of an *address mismatch* would be when a person is attempting to set up, for the very first time, utility services at a new address because he or she has recently relocated.

What you do want to look out for, however, are names and addresses that are completely foreign and unfamiliar to you. This means that someone may have attempted to use your social security number for a credit inquiry. If this happens, it's best to monitor your credit closely, which can be achieved with services such as LifeLock and other identity-theft services.

Fraud Alerts and Personal Statements

A high risk fraud alert may show on a credit report if any of the following has occurred:

- Many recent credit inquiries, which could signify fraudulent attempts for new credit in a short period of time.
- The SSN isn't a standard issued number from the Department of Social Security.
- The address used to obtain the reports appears linked to previous fraudulent activity or is not a residential address.

If you're getting pre-approved for a mortgage, lenders will scrutinize the number of recent inquiries in the most recent 30 to 60 days, to ensure a borrower isn't attempting to acquire too much new credit, too fast.

For the second and third issues, lenders they will request additional SSN verifications (by asking to see your Social Security card, or a letter from the Social Security Administration) and proof of your residential address (with copies of utility bills, mortgage statements or lease agreements).

Finally, if in the most recent two years you've added a personal statement to your credit report, then it will appear in this section.

Consumer personal statements, however, have no real weight toward a credit score and will not overturn any credit decline decisions.

Potentially Negative Items

You may see general descriptions of possible negative factors on a credit report which have no bearing on credit scores.

Sometimes, the information in this section does its best to confuse and worry credit report recipients.

The items listed may also reference prior issues which have since been resolved.

These statements may appear like the following:

- Proportion of balance to available credit limit too high
- Insufficient or lack of credit history
- Previous bankruptcy or foreclosure
- Lien or collection

These statements vary in wording depending on credit reporting company.

When we look at Barry's report we see two of these statements, which means that at some point Barry may have been close to maxed out on his credit cards.

And, we know that Barry once had some sort of derogatory item in the form of a collection or charge-off hit his credit report.

Again, these statements do not impact the actual credit score.

Credit and Trade Lines

This is the most data-heavy area of the credit report.

All of your debts are known as credit and trade lines, and they will be listed here. Any closed or paid-in-full accounts will also appear in this section.

Each tradeline represents a debt—basically any type of loan or credit card for which you've provided a SSN.

Typical tradeline items appearing on a credit report are the following:

- Mortgages
- Home equity loans or lines of credit
- Credit cards
- Merchandise cards (tied to retail brands, i.e., Victoria's Secret, Macy's, Home Depot, Best Buy, Rooms-to-Go, you name it)
- Auto loans or leases
- Student loans

PRO-TIP: Utility services and rental agreements are not listed on credit reports

You may wonder why your mobile phone bill or utility bills, such as your electric, cable and gas bills, aren't reported as trade lines.

Many are shocked when they find out that these items, aren't reflected on their credit reports.

Utility accounts are not items secured by assets, nor can they accrue substantially in their amounts due, like unsecured credit card debt.

Rather, they're tied to services or property for set periods of time, with monthly pay-in-full requirements.

You may just think about them a little differently because the consequences of not paying these items are more tangible.

For example, if you don't pay your power bill, your lights go out.

If you don't pay your rent, you'll get evicted. Not paying your cell phone bill will get you cut off from the rest of the world.

Here are examples of items which do *not* appear on a credit report and are not counted toward credit scores:

- Apartment rents and leases
- Cell phone bills
- Utilities bills, such as electric, gas, water, and so on
- Insurance bills, such as homeowners, auto, or property insurance

Make no mistake that while your payment history on these items isn't reported on a monthly basis, failure to pay them can get you in trouble if they become collections.

Credit and Trade Lines: Getting Granular

Tradelines include the following information:

- Date opened: the date the lines of credit or loans were opened
- Balance: the current amount owed
- Original balance/high limit: the amount of the original loan or the high balance on the card for credit card lines
- Last reported: the most recent reporting

date that the creditor provided any information about the account

- Type: the type of the debt/account—revolving or installment
- Terms: indicates, usually in months or years, the total length of time of the debt. Applies more to installment debts, rather than revolving debts
- Monthly payment: the minimum monthly required payment due
- Status: whether the debt is current or in delinquent standing
- Derogatory: if a debt is in derogatory standing, indicates whether an outstanding payment is 30-, 60-, 90-, or up to 180-days overdue

Credit and Trade Lines

Creditor:
Lexus Financial

Date Opened: 5/13	Balance: $15,402	High Limit: $29,000	Last Reported: 10/14	Type: Installment	Terms: 36
Monthly Payment: $870		Status: On Time	Derogatory:		

Creditor:
Discover

Date Opened: 3/12	Balance: $5,250	High Limit: $9,000	Last Reported: 10/14	Type: Revolving	Terms:
Monthly Payment: $325		Status: On Time	Derogatory:		

Trade and credit lines will appear with full payment histories, minimum monthly payment requirements, status, account details, original open date, terms, and other information. Closed or paid-in-full accounts will also appear here.

We see that Barry first purchased his Lexus back in May 2013 (date opened) for $29,000 (high limit). He secured this debt with an installment loan (type), payable in three years (term).

He currently still owes $15,402 (balance) for which he's making monthly payments of $870 (monthly payment). According to the last reported data, which was in October 2014, he's paying these payments on time (status). Great job, Barry!

On Barry's Discover card, we can see that he's carrying a $5,250 balance out of a $9,000 maximum allowed amount.

He's paying the bill on time according to the latest data, and the minimum monthly payment amount he must send to Discover is $325. Of course, sending in the minimum required amount monthly will take Barry much longer to pay off that whole balance of $5,250.

Finally, we see a closed mortgage from ABC Mortgage on Barry's credit report. According to the last reported data in December 2013, which was probably when it was paid off, Barry had started this mortgage back in May 2006.

The mortgage was originally a 30-year loan, which started at $215,000, and by the time Barry paid it off, likely due to selling the place, the balance was $189,214.

CLOSED

Creditor:
ABC Mortgage

Date Opened:	Balance:	High Limit:	Last Reported:	Type:	Terms:
5/06	$189,124	$215,000	12/13	Installment	360

Monthly Payment:	Status:	Derogatory:
$1,255	PAID IN FULL	

Types of Trade Lines

There are two major types of trade lines: revolving and installment. You may see both on your credit report.

What's the difference between the two?

Revolving: The balances for revolving debts are unsecured, and include credit card debt and lines of credit. "Revolving" debt gets its name simply because balances may rise and fall, and are not secured by, or tied to any assets or things like a house or car.

If we look at Barry's report, we can see that he has a total of four revolving trade lines, or credit card accounts on his credit report: Discover, Chase, Bank of America, and MasterCard.

Installment: The balances for installment loans are tied to secured assets or started at a fixed high loan amount which is to be paid down monthly until it is paid off. Examples of secured assets are houses and cars.

Mortgages are secured by the houses to which they're tied, and car loans are obviously secured by the car.

Every monthly payment toward these types of debts builds more of your share in ownership, or *equity,* and less of the bank's, until one day, that asset is yours free and clear.

Another installment loan example would be a student loan. Your education secured the loan, and unless the balance is renegotiated, every monthly payment made here will decrease the total balance of the original loan.

In Barry's report, we can see that in addition to his revolving debt, he has installment debt in the form of the Lexus auto loan (as we saw previously) and student loan debt from Sallie Mae.

Delinquent and Derogatory Items

Toward the end of the credit report is where most of the negative stuff, such as judgments, liens, bankruptcies, and collections are listed.

For unpaid or late bills, a delinquent status generally appears as soon as an account goes beyond 30-days late. After 180 days the creditor may forward an outstanding debt on to a collection agency.

Who is owed, how much, and when it was owed will also be listed. Creditors report on a monthly basis and accounts will be noted as current or delinquent.

For liens, judgments and civil debts, creditors and collection agencies must be able to verify that any information reported here matches a debtor's name, address, Social Security Number or date of birth.

If they can't, then you have the right to request CRAs to remove this information, according to new credit reporting legislation as of July 2017.

Derogatory Information

COLLECTION:
Con Edison

| Date Opened: | Balance: | Last Reported: |
| 1/10 | $262 | 2/10 |

Monthly Payment: Status:
$25   PAID IN FULL

Public Records, Collections, Charge-offs, Bankruptcies, Foreclosures and any other derogatory information are listed in this section, along with the respective status.

According to Barry's report, looks like he had a collection filed against him by Con Edison, his previous electric provider. But it also looks like it was old (from January 2010) and not for too much money ($262), and that he paid it shortly after it was filed, in February 2010.

Inquiries

Finally, credit reports list any inquiry activity made on the borrower's' behalf, usually within the most recent six months.

An inquiry is logged on a credit report anytime new loans and services are requested, for example, a new credit card application or mortgage or loan prequalification.

It is also possible to see inquiries tied to credit card pre-qualification offers, or utility company credit checks.

Looks like Barry's had four inquiries since 2012, and they were either inquiries for new credit (Capital One, Best Rate Mortgage, Best Buy) or services (Verizon Wireless).

Inquiries	
Capital One	3/2014
Best Rate Mortgage Company	1/2014
Best Buy	1/2013
Verizon Wireless	10/2012

A list of the most recent requests for your credit history. Some reports may provide a more thorough list that separates inquires initiated by you, or by creditors who are screening to make credit offers.

Personal History and Verification Data

Some credit reports will also list a consumer's residential history and name variations.

Lenders may ask that credit applicants verify addresses, and any previous names or aliases used.

They may also compare this data alongside an applicant's verification documents such as a driver's license, passport, social security card, or utility statements showing current addresses.

Putting It All Together

Remember the name mismatch in Barry's file? We can link it to this section as well. Here's where we do a bit of detective work to find out why this name variation exists.

Anytime new credit applications are filed, the personal information—exactly as it was entered to pull the report—is logged.

If the data entered to pull credit contains typos, these are recorded. A log of Barry's name as "Baron" was logged in October 2012. We can look at the inquiries section and link a Verizon Wireless credit with this date.

Personal History and Verification Data			Any addresses, aliases and dates of birth reported by data providers, to further verify consumer information. Name, address or SSN mismatches may also be noted in this section.
Borrower, Barry **AKA** Borrowerz, Barry **NAME MISMATCH** 1/2013	SSN: 234-56-7890		
Borrower, Barry **AKA** Borrower, Baron **NAME MISMATCH** 10/2012	SSN: 234-56-7890		
Current Address: 300 Perry Street New York, NY 10014 Reported 10/2012			
Previous Address: 100 Fulton Street New York, NY 10038 Reported 8/2009	**Previous Address:** 250 Desbrosses Street New York, NY 10013 Reported 10/2006	**Previous Address:** 120 Peachtree Road Atlanta, GA 30324 Reported 10/2006	

Perhaps this was a clerical error on the Verizon data entrant's part. If Barry applied for a new mortgage loan tomorrow, the lender would see these variations and likely ask to see Barry's verification documents to confirm (1) he is who he says he is and (2) the correct spelling of his name compared to what's on his file.

Now that you've got a good understanding of the components of a credit report, let's figure out how credit is scored.

CHAPTER 4:
How Credit is Scored

No matter which method you used to gather your scores, they *should* be pretty similar based on your overall credit history.

If your score is excellent with one bureau, it *should* be reflected this way among the others.

When FICO released information about its scoring models in 2003, it lifted the lid on what factors were used to determine credit score ranges.

So how is credit scored? Let's take a look.

Anatomy of a Score

FICO's model is based on the following factors:

Payment History = 35 Percent

Paying your bills and debts on time has the most significant impact on your credit score and is also the easiest way to start improving your score.

The more recent your late payments, the more negatively it impacts your score.

This is because late payments turn into

collections, charge-offs, and judgments, and these factors also have a significant negative impact on your overall score.

Amounts Owed = 30 Percent

Another name for this simple concept has cropped up in recent years, called the "credit utilization rate."

This factor counts the total amount of credit *used* versus the total amount of credit *available*.

If you're close to being maxed out on your credit cards, then you would have a *high* utilization rate as opposed to someone who carries little to no credit card debt, and has *low* utilization.

Length of Credit History = 15 Percent

This factor takes into consideration how long you've established your credit history across various accounts.

If you've had a long credit history, perhaps with various types of credit over a period of time, then this would be more favorable than if you carried very little or recent credit.

The older your overall credit history, the better. For example, parents with longer credit history would fare better in this area than children with more recent credit history or no credit history at all.

Credit Inquiries = 10 Percent

This factor is determined by the number of inquiries, or requests for new credit, that appear on your credit history within the most recent six to 12 month period.

Credit Mix = 10 Percent

Your credit mix looks at the combination of revolving and installment debt. A mix of auto loans, credit cards, and mortgages would weigh more positively than a concentration of unsecured debt from credit cards alone.

While these are the basic components of the credit score, keep in mind that each CRA tweaks this formula so that it fits their unique models, which is why when you pull the tri-merge report, you should get three *similar* but not *identical* scores.

Myfico.com says, "Each of the three credit reporting agencies probably has different information about you, and that means your scores will also be different. If your information is identical at all three credit reporting agencies, your (FICO) scores should be pretty close."

It's also a fact that the credit scores purchased by consumers are not the same scores used by companies, lenders, and insurers. This is why it's a good idea to simply know where you stand, rather than fixate on the score. Most credit reports these days will also often have an indicator to show you your general risk level.

The Consumer Financial Protection Bureau is aware of the differences between credit scores that consumers receive versus the scores that may be used among industries such as mortgage or insurance.

According to the CFPB, To determine if score variations would lead to meaningful differences between the consumers' and lenders' assessment of credit quality, the [Analysis of Differences between Consumer- and Creditor-Purchased Credit Scores] study divided scores into four credit-quality categories.

The study found that different scoring models would place consumers in the same credit-quality category 73–80 percent of the time.

Different scoring models would place consumers in credit-quality categories that are off by one category 19–24 percent of the time. And from 1 to 3 percent of consumers would be placed in categories that were two or more categories apart.

Which means that the consumer-scoring models, or the excellent, good, fair, or poor categories used to label the majority of credit scores purchased or accessed by consumers, is similar (at roughly 80 percent) to what those industries are seeing when they make their credit decisions. Again, if your score is within good to excellent credit tiers on one report, it should be very similar on others.

So what are the credit tiers?

Excellent	= 750
Good	= 700–749
Average	= 650–699
Bad	= 500–640
Poor	= below 500

According to FICO's Risk of Default calculations, the likelihood of a person with over 750 scores making late payments is less than 2 percent; however, if you have a credit score in the range of 600–649, FICO estimates you may pay bills late roughly 31 percent of the time.

And if you were wondering where most Americans stand, FICO says that the majority of people in the United States have scores just above 700.

FICO® Score Distribution

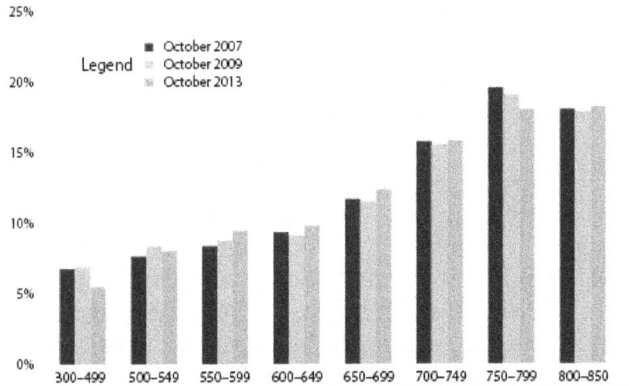

PERCENT OF POPULATION								
FICO® 8 Score	October 2005	October 2006	October 2007	October 2008	October 2009	October 2010	October 2011	October 2012	October 2013
300–499	6.6	6.5	7.1	7.2	7.3	6.9	6.3	6.0	5.8
500–549	8.0	8.0	8.0	8.2	8.7	9.0	8.7	8.5	8.4
550–599	9.0	8.8	8.7	8.7	9.1	9.6	9.9	9.9	9.8
600–649	10.2	10.2	9.7	9.6	9.5	9.5	9.8	10.1	10.2
650–699	12.8	12.5	12.1	12.0	11.9	11.9	12.1	12.2	12.7
700–749	16.4	16.3	16.2	16.0	15.9	15.7	15.5	16.2	16.3
750–799	20.1	19.8	19.8	19.6	19.4	19.5	19.6	18.8	18.4
800–850	16.9	17.9	18.4	18.7	18.2	17.9	18.1	18.4	18.6
TOTAL*	100	100	100	100	100	100	100	100	100

*All columns may not add up to 100.0% due to rounding.

FICO™ Banking Analytics Blog. © 2014 Fair Isaac Corporation.

Notice how, from October 2007 through October 2013, that the percentage of most people with scores over 800 hasn't changed. What *has* changed over the years is the number of people who have fallen out of the 750–799 category and into the score ranges of 550–599, 600–659 (the spread with the most growth during this time period), and 700–749.

This could be attributed to the credit crisis' aftermath since 2007. Perhaps people used more credit cards as backups for emergencies during difficult times. As lending tightened, they may also have turned to unsecured credit card debt for added liquidity. Unemployment may also have prevented many from paying bills on time, impacting their credit scores.

In mortgage lending, if the other components of your qualifying criteria in the form of income and assets look solid, then a credit score above 720 should open up most loan programs to you.

If your score is 760 and above, then that will weigh heavily in your favor, especially considering that most loan underwriting approvals are run through automated systems first and place a lot of emphasis on the middle credit score of the three.

If you're also interested in credit-scoring by state, there is a fantastic interactive credit map at governing.com, also accessible from tccbonline.com. In a nutshell, the top five U.S. states with the best average Experian credit scores are:

Minnesota:	718
North Dakota:	715
South Dakota:	712
Vermont:	712
New Hampshire:	711

How Scores Can Vary

According to a 2011 VantageScore report, most people's scores typically will vary by about 20 points in any 90-day time period which may or may not push you up or down into a different credit score level, and which can make a big difference in interest rates.

Let's now a take deeper look at what specifically drives the inner components behind each credit-scoring factor.

What Scores Like and Don't Like

Now that we have an idea of what factors most impact a credit score, let's do a deeper dive behind each component.

Knowing the underlying methodology behind each component and how they all relate to each other is the knowledge that will give you power to raise your credit score.

Payment History: Pay Your Bills on Time (35 Percent of Credit Score)

You are most rewarded on your credit score for paying all of your bills *on time*. Let me stress this: *pay your bills on time*. Late bill payments also have the most adverse impact on your score.

Your ability to make timely payments says a lot about personal financial responsibility and is crucial to how lenders and companies will determine your eligibility for the loans and services you need.

Within payment history are a number of subfactors of which you should be aware:

Recent late payments hit scores hardest: The most recent 12 months of payment history are most crucial to credit scores.

A single 30-day late payment on any bill can lower scores by as much as 15 to 40 points, and missing payments for all of your bills in the same month can cause a score to tank by 150 points or more! Those 150 points are easy to lose but much harder to gain back.

The greater the lateness, the worse the damage: Once your bills go unpaid past the 30-day mark, and become 60-, 90-, and 180-days late, these consecutive late payments will hurt your score exponentially. What this means is the more and more you fall behind, the more your credit score is dinged. The late payments after the initial 30-days incrementally drive your score downward.

Higher scores take a greater hit: Recent lateness takes more points off excellent than average or bad scores. "For example, for someone with a score over 800, one 30-day late payment can reduce a score by 100 points, whereas someone with a score of 650 may see a change of only 25 points for the same late bill payment."

Chronically late payments should be avoided: Paying late on one bill doesn't look as bad as paying late on all of your bills. Don't allow late bill payments to become a frequency.

Collections, bankruptcies, liens, and judgments: These derogatory items remain on credit scores for up to 10 years. For outstanding collections, the more recent they are, the worse. Very old collection accounts don't hurt scores as much, and eventually, bankruptcies, liens and judgments (if satisfied accordingly) should eventually come off credit reports.

Amounts Owed: Keep Your Balances within Reason (30 Percent of Credit Score)

The balances owed, in proportion to the total credit available has the second greatest impact toward your score. Ideally, you should make an effort to keep your balances as close to or as low as possible compared to the maximum amount allowed.

Cutoffs for Consideration

Credit utilization is ranked in tiers; so understanding the cutoffs for each tier is to your advantage.

Credit utilization tiers based on percentages:

0–19 percent
20–39 percent
40–59 percent
60–79 percent
80–99 percent
100 percent

Each increasing tier harms a score the same as the previous (e.g., if a balance goes from 39 to 40 percent, it will impact the score the same as it would going from 79 to 80 percent). Keep your balances on your revolving accounts (unsecured credit card debt) below 40 percent of the credit limit, and try to never exceed that amount, unless for emergency funds.

It's best to try keeping balances less than 19 percent, which as you can see has the same weight as carrying only 1 percent of the total amount.

Unsecured Debt Is a Killer

In the scoring process, FICO usually looks at the revolving (unsecured credit card) account that is charged closest to its max limit and weighs the heaviest.

It then looks at other revolving accounts, and then installment loan balances, and considers the total amounts owed versus the maximum debt available.

A note about equity lines of credit: If you opened a home equity line of credit (HELOC) recently, know that these are sometimes counted as revolving debt, instead of secured debt collateralized by property.

Unlike a second mortgage, which resembles a standard mortgage because it is an installment loan with a fixed starting balance and term, balances on equity lines of credit can go up or down.

The reason for this? There is support to show that FICO considers low-balance HELOCs up to $10,000 as revolving accounts, whereas those with higher limits upward of $30,000 are treated as second mortgages.

While we can't be sure as to the exact balance tiers, it seems the *amount* of the total credit line deems whether it is revolving or installment debt.

Small Balances Are Better than Zero Balances

Before you pay all your credit cards off and never touch them again, hold on a minute.

While you may think that having zero balances is a surefire strategy for an excellent credit score, the truth is that this tactic doesn't help a score at all.

Only responsible usage of credit—charging and keeping low balances and/or paying for them in full monthly—boosts scores. Utilizing your available credit prudently is good for credit scores.

Length of Credit History (15 Percent of Credit Score)

The third most significant component of credit-scoring is the length of your *overall* credit history as well as the *age* of your individual accounts.

If you have a good, longstanding credit mix, then you'll want to keep these accounts open for as long you can. Here, mortgages, student loans, and anything that requires a long time to pay off will usually help, as well as credit cards that were opened a long time ago and remain open.

Having zero or no credit history will negatively impact you, so the only way to build credit is to use it wisely over time.

Credit Mix (10 Percent of Credit Score)

When it comes to credit, there is such a thing as good or bad credit. The best mix is a combination of secured and unsecured debt, which means a good mix of installment and well-managed revolving debt.

This would look like a mortgage, auto loan or student loan, and credit cards with low balances, and all paid on time.

For perspective: "The average American has 13 credit accounts showing on their credit report, including 9 credit cards and 4 installment loans," according to Fair Isaac.

I learned that FICO picks up on the quality of a debt holder and can recognize when lenders or creditors are bona fide banks, or just finance companies.

Consider this: any merchant or retailers that are always offering same-as-cash deals for a certain period of time (90 days, six months, the first year, and so on) are typically backed by *finance companies*. The offers aren't from banks or prominent creditors such as American Express, Visa, or MasterCard.

FICO picks up on the quality of the credit for which you've qualified, so keep it in mind before you open any new credit.

Inquiries (10 Percent of Credit Score)

Inquiries are logged when any new applications for credit are submitted. Inquiries that result in opening a lot of new accounts in a short period of time can ding your credit score, especially when you have an overall shorter length of credit history.

You're Not Penalized When Rate Shopping for Mortgages

A discrepancy exists here however, and this is when you are getting preapproved for a mortgage.

When you are rate shopping, you can have multiple inquiries up to a 14-day period, and you will only be penalized for one. Also, know that FICO is based on activity for the prior 30 days, so your scores should not be fluctuating while you are rate shopping.

Otherwise, each individual inquiry—up to 10 inquiries—can hurt your credit score by as much as five to 30 points.

Not All Inquiries Are Made Equal

A "soft" pull will not hurt your credit score. Examples of soft credit pulls include those for the following purposes:

Ordering a personal credit report

Setting up utilities (e.g., your water, electric, gas, and cable services)

Receiving prescreened or preapproved credit card solicitations and offers

Prescreening for employment purposes

Credit monitoring

Recent Credit Scoring Changes

Lien and Civil Debt Records Must Be Accurate

Starting July 2017, credit reporting rules changed, and the CRAs will remove and exclude tax liens and civil debts if any negative information does not include a customer's name, address and Social Security Number or date of birth.

In 2011 alone, the CFPB reported 8 million complaints about wrong information in credit reports were received by the three major credit-reporting firms. And in 2012 the FTC revealed that 21% of consumers had a verified error in their credit reports.

After all, if creditors can't keep track of who

owes them money, then they shouldn't be able to file negative information on your credit report.

Medical Debts Get Softer Treatment

If your credit score suffered due to past due medical debts, 2015's new rules tilt in your favor.

Because medical debts take so long to process and pay (whether it's you or the insurance companies paying), the CFPB now offers more time to sort this out by granting a new 180-day grace period for medical debt repayment.

For paid past due medical debts only, the new rule also states that once these debts are paid, they will disappear from your credit report entirely. In the past, even you paid off past due debt, it could remain for years.

CHAPTER 5:
How to Correct Errors on Credit Reports

When checking your credit report, scrutinize each section.

Log any and all inaccuracies and items up for dispute on a separate worksheet, spreadsheet, or notepad.

If you're working with a tri-merged report, remember to note the respective CRA with the information to be disputed.

You wouldn't want to dispute negative information with Equifax if only TransUnion is showing the negative information.

Checking Your Credit Report for Errors

Personal Information

Check to ensure that all personal identifying information is correct, such as your full name, address, social security number (when disclosed), and birth date. Note if there are any variations at the beginning and anywhere else in the report.

Minor name or address mismatches are

common, such as misspellings or omissions of parts of names such as middle names or hyphen-ated names. Incomplete or misspelled addresses, incorrect apartment numbers or postal codes are also common.

If you find any significant personal identifying information that is completely unrecognizable to you, make a note of the dates linked with these variations.

This could indicate that someone else with similar information to yours has previously applied for credit, and/or these are just inaccuracies that need to be removed. In extreme cases, unrecogniz-able personal information combined with unrecog-nizable accounts means that someone may have used your identity or social security number to open new credit accounts.

Credit and Trade Lines

Scan your credit and trade lines very carefully. Look for the following:

Accounts you don't recognize.

Negative or delinquent information. This includes late payments, statuses (on time vs. delinquent, open vs. paid-in-full, etc.) collections, charge-offs, judgments, liens, and bankruptcies. If you've left any unsecured credit card debts unpaid for more than six months, then your accounts past the 180-day late mark may convert to charge-offs. This means that the creditor has charged off the debt from its books and decided it is unlikely to receive any sort of payment on the debt. Also be mindful of very recent versus very old derogatory information.

Any cosigned or joint accounts. Confirm your status on these.

Inaccurate balances. Check that your maximum charged or allowable balances on revolving accounts are correct. Note where they are inaccurate. Remember that most lenders or banks report 30 days in arrears, so if you've made any recent and significant payments to reduce balances this activity may have not yet posted.

Note: If your name is very similar to someone else's in your family, for example, your father is Bob Jones Sr. and you are Bob Jones Jr., in some cases your credit data may be mixed together. While technology and reporting has improved here in recent years, this is still a common occurrence, and any inaccuracies should be corrected.

Inquiries

When reviewing your credit report, ensure that you recognize the most recent credit inquiries.

Pay particular attention to any unrecognizable inquiries, because these are the types tied to applications for new credit.

Ensure that any new inquiries showing are indeed yours. Also, look for any inquiries from over two years ago. These can usually be removed upon request.

If you don't recognize the companies by either names or addresses, then you have a right to dispute them and have them removed. An unauthorized inquiry without your express request or permission is a violation according to the FCRA.

Crosscheck Your Reports

Depending on which methods you used to obtain your report, you may have one tri-merge report that has consolidated all three CRAs' records, or you may have separate information across three single reports.

In both cases, determine whether negative information is reported by only one CRA as opposed to the other two, and vice versa. Any discrepancies should be flagged.

The Dispute Process

If you've found your credit report to be accurate in total, Congratulations! If not, then let's work to remove any negative or inaccurate information you found.

It is important to understand that in some cases you may be successful at removing negative information showing on your credit report *even if it is yours*.

This process is detailed in the next section, which includes submitting a written dispute and resolution request with the possibility that the negative information can be removed.

A 2013 FTC report estimated that one out of every five people has an inaccurate credit report. On a national scale, that translates to as many as 42 million mistakes.

If you wish to remove negative items from your credit reports, you'll need to follow the dispute resolution request process. Requests are made in a formal written process, in which you will submit letters to the CRAs or creditors stating which negative items you wish to have removed from your credit reports.

From the time of the receipt of the letters, the CRAs have 30 days to take action. If you find erroneous information you'll follow the same process, either requesting a removal of the item (e.g., collection that is not yours) or a correction (e.g., request that a late payment be corrected to timely).

Use the template letters in this chapter for this process. You may have received dispute letter forms included with your credit reports. You can also refer to sample dispute resolution letters in this book which you can also download at tccbonline.com.

> **PRO-TIP:** You should provide as little information as possible regarding your personal account information—you shouldn't even reference the credit report ID or enclose a copy of the CRA's credit report, because by doing so, you are only facilitating the reinvestigation process timeline.
>
> Forcing the CRAs to start from scratch with no information makes the 30 day clock tick in your favor, but it's up to you. I've been successful at removals using both methods.

Remember to stay organized during this process. Track your progress by keeping a worksheet of the trade lines being disputed, as well as the dates when letters are sent.

Keep copies of everything, and never send in original copies of anything.

Remember, from the time requests are made, the CRAs are required to respond or remove negative and inaccurate information within 30 days.

Reinvestigation and Reverification

The formal terms to request that negative items be removed from credit files are "reinvestigation" and "reverification." These are terms used only by the CRAs and those in the credit reporting industries.

They are essentially the same as a standard investigation and verification, but because credit reporting agencies consider any compiling of a report to be an investigation, they therefore refer to the process of verifying that data as a *re*-investigation.

You'll see these terms referenced throughout the template letters in this chapter, and available for free download at tccbonline.com.

Adverse and Negative Items

While the laws vary from state to state concerning statute of limitations on credit report items, for most states the rule is seven years.

This means that that adverse information regarding bankruptcies, collections, tax liens, judgments, some civil suits, and some child support debts are on file for at least seven years.

Hard inquiries remain on credit records for two years. That said, many have been successful at removing negative information from showing up at all on their credit reports, *even if it was theirs*.

"Even when an item is accurate, dispute the information, since it costs almost nothing. There's always a chance that disputing entries can work," according to Dana Neal, author of "Best Credit."

Sometimes, either due to faulty record keeping or noncontact by an original creditor or collection agency, the CRAs simply can't verify adverse items within the allowed 30-day time frame; therefore, by default they *must* remove them.

This dispute process is the starting point to removing negative information, and many will find that they can do so successfully, using the sample letters in this chapter, by having the CRAs remove the following items from their credit report:

Bankruptcies: If you're attempting to remove a bankruptcy before the end of the standard seven-year reporting period, you'll have a better shot at it after at least two years from when it was discharged, and after you've disputed and removed any and all debts that were settled as part of your bankruptcy.

Collections: If the bureau cannot verify that the collection is legitimate within the reinvestigation time frame set forth by the FCRA (30 days), then the law requires that it be removed from your report.

Collections are often reported by service bureaus, which are notorious for making mistakes, including transcribing SSNs incorrectly; if the CRA is able to provide verification documentation, ensure that it has recorded all information accurately, since any errors are cause for deletion.

Judgments: Attempt to dispute these; otherwise you may have to arrange a settlement with the plaintiff. A paid judgment is far better on a credit record than an unpaid one.

Tax Liens: While you may be successful in having

a tax lien removed from your credit report with a standard dispute process, if you actually paid the tax lien in full and it was under $25,000, then recent news indicates that the IRS may be agreeable in removing this item from your credit report. You may not fare so well if the tax lien is greater than this amount, and it is unpaid.

> **PRO-TIP**: Remember that as of July 2017, if the creditor cannot verify the accuracy of your personal information and the debt does not include a customer's name, address, SSN or date of birth, then they cannot report it.

Inquiries: Hard inquiries ding your credit score. Dispute them to have them removed, especially if you don't recognize them. Remember that if you're rate shopping for a mortgage this shouldn't hurt your credit score within a 30-day timeframe.

Prescreened offers also won't ding your scores, as these are considered soft pulls.

Target Erroneous Items

In addition to disputing adverse items, you'll want to dispute negative items that aren't yours at all.

Do not confuse this with disputing adverse information, which concerns the entire deletion of a negative item.

For example, if you have a credit card trade line showing a late payment that you want to dispute, you wouldn't want to have the entire trade line removed from your report. You'd just want the late payment corrected if you have proof of timely payment.

Dispute in Writing, Not Online

Earlier on in Chapter 2, I mentioned that it's best to request your free annual credit reports in writing to be delivered by mail from each of the three CRAs.

Not only does this give you a complete picture of what each bureau has on file for you, but it also prevents you from being subject to any limitations of liability and arbitration agreements that you must agree to when obtaining online reports.

When disputing negative information and requesting resolutions on credit reports, the same holds true.

Online forms are notorious for forcing consumers to pigeonhole their disputes in irrelevant categories and for forcing consumers to sacrifice certain legal rights.

Don't let online convenience distract you from the recommended snail mail procedure.

From a Fox Business Network article in 2013:

Sending in a dispute online may be quick. However, consumer lawyers say it's one of the biggest mistakes you can make.

> "The online dispute is all about the expediency of the credit bureau," says Cary Flitter, a consumer lawyer and law professor in Philadelphia. Most online dispute forms give you just enough room to state your

dispute, he says, but don't give you enough room to back it up.

"They want you to just say, 'not mine' or 'bill was paid,' and that doesn't always tell the whole story," says Flitter.

Online disputes are also not setup to accept additional evidence, such as a copy of a check or of your Social Security card, say experts—and those pieces of evidence can be important later on if you do need to go to court to prove that a credit reporting agency isn't correcting a legitimate mistake.

In addition, many online dispute forms contain arbitration clauses, which can undercut your consumer rights. "The credit bureaus bury waiver clauses in the click agreement," says Flitter. "By clicking, 'I accept,' you're giving up the right to sue them if they do something wrong."

Type up, then mail your dispute instead. That way, you can include as much information and evidence as you need to explain your case. Also, if you do wind up in court, you'll be able to prove to the judge assigned to your case that you gave the credit bureaus enough information to properly investigate your dispute.

As mentioned above, send in your dispute letters by mail.

Better, send them by certified mail, or with delivery confirmation, so you can ensure your documents were received.

Keep copies of your dispute letter and all enclosures. Write the certified mail number on each letter so that you can easily match the certified letter confirmation with the original dispute.

The Magic Number: 30 Days

Credit reporting companies must reinvestigate the items in question within 30 days.

During this period, the bureau will set out to ask the creditor if the disputed information is correct or false.

> According to an article in the *Chicago Sun Times*,
>
> "This is not a human process, but is computerized. One computer is querying another. Essentially, credit bureaus are just warehouses reflecting information collected from creditors; they just report what creditors tell them.
>
> "It's garbage in, garbage out," says credit expert John Ulzheimer.
>
> If the creditor agrees the information is wrong, the information will be corrected on all. You shouldn't need to repeat the procedure with the other bureaus. If a creditor says disputed information is accurate, the information remains on your report with the bureau. If a creditor doesn't respond within the required 30 days, the information is supposed to be removed."

The simple fact is that consumer dispute letters have high levels of success because creditors are too busy to contact the CRAs to verify information before the end of the time frame allowed!

If the CRAs can't verify derogatory information, by law they *must remove it*.

Knowing this, you have nothing to lose by

requesting to have negative information removed from your credit report.

Minimize or Separate Your Disputes per Letter

If you have multiple items to dispute, don't try to dispute all of them together.

Disputing single items or no more than two items at a time is the best practice.

Use the applicable dispute template letter for no more than two errors at a time. For additional disputes, mail those in separately on separate dispute letters. The likelihood of fixing your credit is better if the CRAs handle your disputes one at a time.

Again, stay organized. If you are disputing a negative item that is showing only on a single CRA's report, for example, an account that is present on your Equifax report and not your Experian report, you send in the dispute letter to the correct CRA.

While the CRAs aren't obligated to notify each other, they may at times communicate with each other regarding inaccurate information to be removed. You wouldn't want to cause further confusion for negative information that's not there.

Send Your Letters to CRAs and the Original Creditor

If you know which lender, collection agency, or other type of data furnisher (the ones giving out your information) is misreporting your credit history, send them the same information that you sent the credit bureau.

This procedure ensures that data furnishers

have enough information to investigate your dispute.

According to the consumer lawyer Cary Flitter in the FBN report,

> "That's another reason to do paper disputes because you're going to be caught in the middle." The credit bureaus process your dispute by assigning a category code to the dispute and sending a short summary to the furnisher to investigate the problem. If creditors don't respond, according to the CFPB website, you can also log complaints with the Consumer Financial Protection Bureau.
>
> After we forward your complaint, the company has 15 days to respond to you and the CFPB. Companies are expected to close all but the most complicated complaints within 60 days.
>
> You'll be able to review the response and give us feedback. If we find that another agency would be better able to assist, we will forward your complaint and let you know.
>
> We also share complaint data with state and federal agencies who oversee financial products and services, and we publish a database of non-personal complaint information so the public knows what kinds of complaints we receive and how companies respond."

Follow the Formula

The most effective dispute letters are often the easiest to read.

Don't try to incite legal arguments or use confusing, fake legalese, or other fancy phrases and words. Many letters that have been posted online as samples don't make sense, are ineffective, and will get you nowhere.

In other words, stick to the letters in this chapter which are available for free for you to download at tccbonline.com.

Instead, a brief, pointed dispute letter that states politely in plain English what the error is and what you want done about it is best. You need to be clear about what you're disputing and are entirely in your right to say, "The account was never mine," or "The payment was never late."

The letter must come directly from you, the consumer, to trigger credit bureau obligations for investigation. Luckily, the mystery's been taken out of writing these letters from scratch and template letters are provided for your use below.

Include Evidence, Only if It Helps

When sending in dispute requests, only include evidence when it will support your case.

If you're disputing collections and negative information that don't belong to you, then obviously no documentation will be available.

When it helps your dispute, include documentation.

Late Payment Dispute

Include copies of monthly creditor account statements showing your payments posted in a timely manner from one month to the next without late fees.

Another example of supporting documentation could be copies of excerpts from your checking account statements, showing the dates of outgoing bill payments, or if paid with check, a copy of the front and back images of the cashed check.

If you dealt a creditor concerning your issue, it helps to include a statement typed out on a separate letter detailing any specific dates, times, and with whom you spoke at the company.

Collection Status Dispute

If you're trying to correct a status of a collection to "Paid in Full," include the respective template letter plus proof of payment of the collection with the cashed-check copy as well as any agency statement for reference.

You're asking the CRA to contact the original creditor or collection agency for verification, so provide proof if possible. Remember to keep copies of everything that you send, and certify or track those deliveries.

Don't rely on the CRAs and other parties to keep track of your documentation and support your disputes.

"Many court cases turn on the extent of the information that the credit bureau gives the furnisher. The credit bureau will say, 'customer claims paid,' but they will never attach a copy of the check," says Cary Flitter, the consumer lawyer from the FBN report.

"The credit bureaus rarely include the documents you mailed with your dispute (when they are reverifying), and so the furnisher only gets the bare minimum of information. It's up to you to have this information on the ready."

The Dispute Letters

The sample letters provided are for you to repurpose as your own. These letters are also available for download at www.tccbonline.com.

They provide areas for you to list the item(s) you are disputing and also reference timing and your rights under the FCRA.

1. Demand Removal of Inaccurate Information, CRA (First Letter)
This letter is for credit reporting agencies. It is to be used the first time you request inaccurate or adverse information to be removed from your credit report.

[date]

RE: Reporting of Negative and/or Inaccurate Creditor Information

To Whom It May Concern:

I formally request that the following inaccurate and negative items be immediately reinvestigated. They are not indicative of my true credit history. In accordance with 15 USC section 1581i of the Fair Credit Reporting Act, I demand that these items be re-verified and deleted from my record:

Item No.	Creditor	Account Number	Comments
1	*Sample Creditor*	*0000-0000-0000*	*Remove late payment information. Account has never been paid late.*
2	*Sample Creditor*	*0000000*	*Remove this account. Does not belong to me.*

By reporting this information, my ability to obtain new credit is jeopardized. Please see the enclosed credit report for reference.

This is a formal notice, and I expect your compliance of my request, as well as a copy of the corrected report provided to me, within 30 days.

Sincerely,

[Your Full Name]
[Last four of SSN] [Credit Report Reference ID, Code or Number - *optional*]
[Your Address]

2. Demand for Removal of Inaccurate Information (Second Letter)

*This letter is for credit reporting agencies. It is to be used the second time, or thirty days after
your first request for inaccurate or adverse information to be removed from your report.*

[date]
RE: Reporting of Inaccurate Creditor Information
To Whom It May Concern:

On [first letter date], you received my letter disputing inaccurate and adverse items on my
credit report. The original letter is enclosed.

Your negligence has caused me harm, since it has affected my ability to [specify the harm it has
caused, such as "obtain new credit"].

Under the Fair Credit Reporting Act 15 USC 1681i(5)(A), you had 30 days from receipt of this
letter to respond to my request for reverification of the erroneous items. Since I have not
received a reply from you within these 30 days, the information was either inaccurate or could
not be reverified, thus according to provisions 15 USC section 1681i(a), the items must be
deleted immediately.

Please respond to prevent my pursuing my legal rights under 15 USC 1681n or 1781x, which
require your compliance with the law.

Also, pursuant to 15 USC 16891i(d) of the Fair Credit Reporting Act, please send me notice of
the removal of the inaccurate and adverse items, and a revised credit report to the address
below. According to the provisions of 15 USC section 1681j, there should be no charge for
notification of changes on my credit report.

Sincerely,

[Your Full Name]
[Last four of SSN] [Credit Report Reference ID, Code or Number - *optional*]
[Your Address]

3. Demand for Removal of Inaccurate Information (Subsequent Letter)

This letter is for credit reporting agencies. It is to be used for subsequent requests for inaccurate or adverse information to be removed from your report.

[date]

RE: Reporting of Inaccurate Creditor Information

To Whom It May Concern:

On [first letter date], you received my first certified letter disputing inaccurate and adverse items on my credit report. On [second letter date], another request was made for reinvestigation. The original letters are enclosed.

Under the Fair Credit Reporting Act 15 USC 1681i(5)(A), you had 30 days from receipt of the letter to respond to my request for reverification of the erroneous items.

Your negligence has caused me harm, since it has affected my ability to [specify the harm it has caused, such as "obtain new credit"].

Since you have not provided names of persons you contacted for reverification, per 15 USC 1681i6Biii, nor complied within the statutory period of 30 days, I assume that you have not been able to reverify the information I have disputed. Therefore, you must comply with the provision 15 USC section 1681i(a) of the Fair Credit Reporting act and remove the disputed items from my credit report immediately.

If I do not receive a revised credit report, free of charge, with the items removed at the address below, I will pursue my legal rights with an attorney under 15 USC section 1681n or 1681o "Civil liability for willful noncompliance." Your credit bureau may be liable for:

1) actual damaged I sustained by your failure to delete the items
2) punitive damages as the court may allow
3) costs of the court action, plus attorney's fees

I have forwarded a copy of this letter to the Consumer Financial Protection Bureau.

Sincerely,

[Your Full Name]
[Last four of SSN] [Credit Report Reference ID, Code or Number]
[Your Address]

4. Demand For a Credit Bureau to Remove Inquiry

This letter is for CRAs when demanding that they remove an unauthorized inquiry from your report.

[date]

RE: Remove Unauthorized Inquiries

To Whom It May Concern:

I recently received a copy of my credit file and noticed that there are unauthorized inquiries on it.

[If you know that the inquiry was intended for review purposes only, and *not* for an application for new credit, state it here, e.g., "I have not made any applications for new credit on the inquiry date   listed."]

This has hurt my chances of obtaining new credit. I demand that you remove the following inquiries immediately:

[List All:]
[name of creditor]
[date of inquiry]
[subscriber or reference code, if there is one]

Consider this a formal notice. I expect your compliance of my request by rules according to the Fair Credit Reporting Act, as well as a copy of the corrected report provided to me within 30 days.

Sincerely,

[Your Full Name]
[Your Address]
[Last four of SSN]

5. Demand for Creditor Removal of Inaccurate Information

This letter is for creditors only. Send it when demanding that they update or remove inaccurate and adverse information.

[date]

RE: [Reporting of Inaccurate Information, Your Full Account Number]

To Whom It May Concern:

Enclosed you'll find a copy of my credit report. The report contains the following false information: [state the false information, such as "30-day late payment in November 2014"].

I demand that you instruct the credit bureaus to remove this negative information immediately and notify me with a copy of this instruction.

By reporting this information, you are in violation of the Fair Credit Reporting Act. This is hurting me [state how it is hurting you, such as "by damaging my credit score thus resulting in my inability to obtain favorable credit"], and I expect your compliance within 30 days according to the Fair Credit Reporting Act.

Sincerely,

[Your Full Name]
[Last four of SSN]
[Your Address]

Credit Dispute Letter 1: Use the first letter on your first attempt at disputing inaccurate or adverse information on your credit report with the CRAs. There is reference to an enclosed CRA-generated credit report, however you aren't obligated to include a copy of a report.

Credit Dispute Letter 2 (follow-up): Use on your second attempt, or 30 days after the first letter, if you haven't received any response from the CRAs regarding your first dispute.

Credit Dispute Letter 3 (subsequent): Hopefully you won't have to use the third letter, but use it if you don't hear anything from the CRAs after your second letter.

It's highly unlikely that you won't hear something within 30 days, but this letter is here just in case. It has stronger language and mentions the possibility that you will pursue legal action for noncompliance.

Creditor Dispute Letter Request: Use this letter to contact creditors directly about removing inaccurate or adverse information they are reporting to the CRAs.

You can submit this at the same time you submit your letter to the CRA.

Credit Inquiry Removal Request: Use this letter to contact CRAs about removing a hard pull credit inquiry which you don't recognize, and which may negatively impact your credit score.

Once you've submitted your dispute letters, you should receive written notification of any CRA or creditor resolution within 30 days.

I have been successful at having negative, adverse, and inaccurate information removed or corrected, because the CRAs were unsuccessful at reverifying the negative information with the original creditors.

Try it for yourself. You have nothing to lose (except the cost of a first-class stamp) and everything to gain including a higher credit score.

Fraud Alerts and Credit Freezes

If you are certain you've been a victim of identity theft, then you can place a fraud alert on your own credit report to dissuade creditors from issuing any new credit.

The fraud alert itself, in most cases, won't prevent the issuance of new credit; rather, it will provide a red flag to hopefully alert the lender to re-verify an applicant's identification.

Identification should be verified with documents such as a driver's license, passport, social security card, or even a residential history, to prove that the person requesting the new credit is in fact, the right person.

This was the protocol when I worked in the mortgage industry, as fraud alerts were quite common on credit reports. When this occurred, extra underwriting conditions were required prior to full loan approval, such as the above-mentioned verification of identification or residential history with documentation.

Some states will allow for consumers to place credit freezes on their personal files, which prevents anyone from opening an account in your name. This could help if you suspect that anyone, even an ex-spouse, is using your personal information to open a new account in your name.

A vengeful ex-spouse could file a bankruptcy in

your name because many districts don't require identification when a bankruptcy is first filed. These types of criminal bogus filings will get recorded as public records.

Believe it or not, vengeful people are capable of performing such a filing, and you'll have to seek a bankruptcy attorney to get the filing expunged; let's hope that bankruptcy attorneys would know to verify identifications before it got this far.

If you can't place a credit freeze on your report, then the fraud alert would be your best alternative bet.

CHAPTER 6:
How to Improve Your Credit Scores

When it comes to credit scores, I've shown you the factors that weigh the most in determining your score.

Credit scores are generated from complex mathematical formulas and algorithms that weigh and measure these factors against each other.

We can manage our behaviors to raise our credit scores outside of monitoring and keeping our credit reports error-free.

Here are ways to improve your credit scores without resorting to debt management or credit repair services.

Immediate Hacks to Boost Your Score

Listed below are immediate ways to boost your credit score, based on strategies that speak directly to credit scoring factors (Chapter 4).

You may not be able to tackle all of the methods at once, but being strategic about your execution will give you an advantage over stressing out and doing nothing at all.

With a little organization and an empowered, educated approach, you can avoid costly debt counseling or debt repair services which don't often always help you, nor do they get you to a better place than you were before.

With responsible credit management, you can typically improve your score 10 to 15 points in just a few months, which can definitely push you up into a higher credit level when you're on the edge.

These are my best bets to hack and game the credit scoring system.

Bring Delinquent (Pre-collection) Debts Current

This is different from long-term practices concerning collections, which I'll discuss later.

Remember that payment history is the biggest factor of your credit score, so if you have any outstanding loan or credit card debts right now that are currently past due, try to bring them current, before they get to charge-off or collection status.

Scores will drop steepest and fastest in the month following a negative credit event such as missing a payment.

The higher your current credit score, the greater the impact of a single late payment.

But once you bring the payment current, your credit score will recuperate fairly quickly and in some cases, as evidenced by a Credit Sesame writer who paid a bill late on purpose, only to bring it current quickly, her credit score actually improved by over 130 points from 705 to over 736 after she brought her debt current.

Pay Down Your Debt by Credit Scoring Tier

Remember that credit is scored in tiers.

How maxed out you are on your credit cards accounts for a third of your total score, so be strategic about how much you allocate toward your debts.

Check back to Chapter 4 to remind yourself of the credit scoring tiers.

If you're trying to pay down your credit card debt, then pay them down by credit scoring tier. For example, if you have a credit card total limit of $10,000, try to keep your balance at *under* 40% ($4,000) or *under* 20% ($2,000).

Your credit score won't likely change if you keep your balance anywhere between $2,001 to $4000, but it will increase if you keep your balance below $1,999. Do this for each of your credit cards.

Request Increases to Your Credit Lines

If you can't pay down your credit card debts right away, then try requesting increases to your credit lines. Doing so will improve the percentages of your credit used versus your total credit limit available, known as credit utilization ratios.

Don't Apply for New Credit

Stop applying for new credit. Period. New credit applications negatively impact two factors of credit scoring: inquiries (10%) and length of overall credit history (15%). The inquiries will be recorded on your credit report the new debt will bring down the overall average age of your of your credit.

Don't Close Your Old Credit Card Accounts

Just like you should avoid opening new credit, you should keep any older credit accounts open, to contribute to a longer overall credit history.

With loans, you obviously can't keep those open because once you've paid off a car loan, for example, then that's it. But if you can keep your credit card accounts open, then you should. The exception here is if you absolutely won't use them again, in the case of merchandise or retail cards, that will only tempt you to get into debt that you cannot manage responsibly.

Charge Small Items, Pay Them Off In the Next Billing Cycle

Remember that credit scoring also values responsible credit usage and activity.

For credit cards, holding a zero balance isn't a surefire strategy for an excellent credit score; in fact this tactic doesn't help or hurt your score.

Only responsible usage of credit—charging and keeping low balances and/or paying for them in full monthly—boosts scores. A recommendation here would be using a credit card to pay a monthly utility, and being sure to pay that credit card balance in full according to your billing cycle and statement. Utilizing your available credit prudently is good for credit scores.

Long-Term Best Practices

Pay Bills on Time

The single-handed easiest and fastest way to boost your credit scores is to pay your bills on time.

Timely bill payment has the most weight toward credit scoring, so do your best at staying on top of paying your bills on time.

Remember, late bill payments ding higher scores more than lower scores, so it's harder to build an excellent score back once it's hit with a late payment.

Also remember that late payments are logged on credit reports only *after* they are 30 days past due, so you can relax if you missed your payment by a couple of days. Don't get into this habit, however, because late payments on credit cards may translate into higher finance charges overall.

Creditors always note in the fine print that once late payments are logged, your APRs may go up, so be very careful about paying your bills on time.

Challenge Late Fees

As eager as they are to hit you with late fees and higher finance charges, creditors can also be somewhat forgiving if you call in to request a late fee to be waived.

Just like the ball is in your court to maintain an accurate credit record, it's your responsibility to dispute late fees.

I've been successful at having late fees removed when I've requested this from creditors, and my paying my bills on time probably helps with these requests.

Explain that you missed your payment because you were on vacation, or that you simply forgot this one time (if you are a timely-paying customer, stress this point), and the creditor will likely waive your late fee.

Set Up Payment Alerts

Technology now assists in so many ways by reminding you of bill payments when due.

Also, not receiving a monthly paper statement does not mean you can skip that payment. Your agreement with the creditor is that you will repay your debt or the minimum amount due by the due date, so try to get it in on time.

Set up e-mail or text payment reminders. Auto-schedule your bill payments. If you have a mobile app for your creditor, allow a push notification on payment date.

Keep Your Older Accounts Open

If you've got older credit cards with high credit lines, keep those accounts open. The older, the better. The smaller the amount charged against the maximum allowed, the better.

The length of your overall credit history accounts for 15 percent of your credit score, so keeping your older accounts open is a good idea.

This also helps your overall credit utilization rate, the second highest contributing factor to your credit score.

If you are desperate to decrease the amount of credit cards you have, only close out merchant cards, such as retail cards that were offered at the time you were buying something—if you know you're unlikely to use them again.

Add to this any cards with small available credit lines that you're probably not going to use again— the older cards with the higher credit limits matter more.

Forget About Older Derogatory Accounts

The more recent a negative item, the more damage it is doing to your credit score. As negative items age, they have less of an impact on a credit score.

For one negative credit behavior (and no other negative events are added to the report), its impact diminishes over time. For additional negative events, the score will continue to drop.

Years ago, it was ill-advised to pay off older collections beyond three years old because payment would then log a more recent reporting date and bring the collection back from the dead, ultimately hurting your credit scores.

While the CRAs will say that they have improved this conundrum by working with collection agencies, I simply wouldn't take the risk. Some have referred to this as the creditor "dusty pile" or simply put, "letting sleeping dogs lie."

It is also a bad idea to pick up the phone and call on collection agencies regarding your old collections.

Collection agencies, through a tactic called "re-aging" will sometimes bring a file back from the dead and restart the statute clock once any new activity has been received, including offers to settle.

While this is illegal, don't initiate it—imagine

how delighted the collection agency would be to dust off your file when it has already assumed it won't receive anything for the debt.

Let me be clear—this isn't advice to not pay your debts; this is simply the truth when it comes to maintaining and improving your credit score.

Stop Buying Things on Credit

If you've got a spending problem, then it's time to rein in the expenses. The more you spend on credit, the more debt you accrue.

I've resorted to some pretty extreme measures to avoid spending on credit which include leaving the credit cards at home (which means I can't splurge), cutting up credit cards (which means I can't use physically use them), and unlinking them from smartphone wallet apps (which means I must pay in cash or by debit card).

Mind Your Balances

Pay your balances in full monthly, or keep them low. Remember that 15 percent of a credit score was due to the total credit utilized, or amount owed versus the amount of total available credit.

How much debt you carry month to month on your unsecured debt—debt on credit cards—has a significant impact on your credit score.

If you can keep these balances as low as possible, preferably under 30 percent of your total credit, then your credit score will be healthier than if you were being close to maxed out. For example, if you have a $10,000 credit limit, then it's ideal to not carry a balance of more than $3,000 from statement to statement.

I realize that for those who currently have high credit card debt, this may not be feasible, at least not for a while.

But you can chip away at your debt slowly, paying over and above your monthly finance charges to get your balances down.

Carrying very small balances on your credit cards from month to month, as long as you pay the amount due by the due date won't hurt. I'm talking about carrying less than 5 percent of the total balance, not leaving your balances close to maxed out, if you can help it. Monthly credit usage stimulates reporting and history and also shows credit management.

Ideally, paying off the full amounts charged every month will save you the most money from high credit card finance charges anywhere in the range of the 14 to 20 percent mark, and you'll be helping out your credit score a great deal.

Pay Down Your Debt at Lower Costs

In some cases, it may be beneficial to move debt to a 0% APR card that you can payoff within a certain amount of time. Another option could be to consolidate unsecured debt with a fixed loan at a lower APR.

Your goal here is to not shift debt around, but to actually make a dent in it.

If you have high credit card debt, consider consolidating your high-interest debt with credit cards offering zero interest fees for transferred balances, and zero interest on new purchases for a period of time.

While I wouldn't normally recommend the shifting around of debt, taking advantage of credit offers with introductory zero percent APR periods (the longer the better) can provide an opportunity for your payments will have a more significant impact on balance reduction.

Mix Up Your Credit

Manage your mix of unsecured (considered bad if you carry high balances) and secured debt (better because it's tied to assets).

If you've got a couple of credit cards, an auto loan, and a student loan, then that's a pretty diverse mix. Utilize the cards by charging small balances and paying them in full monthly and continue paying timely on those installment loans.

Credit scoring favors good credit usage and behaviors, so you'll want to keep your accounts open and paid timely.

Some people make the mistake of not using their credit cards at all; however, if you carry little to no credit card debt, resume small amounts of charging activity to boost your score. Just remember to pay all bills on time.

Limit New Credit Applications

Don't obtain new credit unless you absolutely must do so.

Each new credit card application counts as a hard pull, which hurts your credit. It also results in brand new credit being logged, which re-ages your overall combined length of credit history.

Just say "No thanks," the next time you're asked if you'd like to open a new credit account because "it will save you x percentage on your total purchases for that day."

Ask yourself, "Do I really need to open this card?"

If you had intended to pay cash, then do so. Or use an existing credit card, and pay your purchases off timely. Opening new merchant accounts not only tempts you to spend more, but also runs the risk of leaving credit balances longer and subject to interest fees.

Opt-Out: It's Your Right

If you don't want creditors and banks prescreening your credit without your knowledge and don't want solicitations for credit card and/or loan offers, then dial the National Opt-Out hotline or submit your request via the online opt-out form.

Creditors and financial institutions pre-screen consumer credit records for the purposes of short-listing a target group to send prescreened credit card offers.

If you've got credit, then your name is already on a marketing list, and you're likely being checked for your credit usage and total credit utilization. If you've got excellent credit because you carry very little credit card debt, you may be solicited for credit cards with the best or lowest annual percentage rates (APRs).

Creditors can also see if you're carrying a lot of consumer debt, and you may then be shortlisted for a credit card that offers a low or 0 percent interest rate on transferred balances.

But what if you don't want to receive prescreened credit offers? If you're deluged with these offers and want them to stop, you have the right to opt out. Here's the information from the Federal Trade Commission and on the related ftc.gov webpage.

You can opt out of receiving them for five years or opt out of receiving them permanently.

To opt out for five years: Call toll-free *opt-out* (1-888-567-8688) or visit optoutprescreen.com.

To opt out permanently: You may begin the permanent opt-out process online at optoutpre-screen.com. To complete your request, you must return the signed *permanent opt-out election form*, which will be provided after you initiate your online request.

When you call or visit the website, you'll be asked to provide certain personal information, including your home telephone number, name, social security number, and date of birth. The infor-mation you provide is confidential and will be used only to process your request to opt out.

While you may wish to stop receiving these kinds of offers in the mail, especially if you're not in the market for a new credit card or insurance policy, or want to stop mailbox clutter, remember that you'll also be missing out on many benefits of learning about what's available, comparing costs, and finding the best product for your needs.

The terms of prescreened offers also may be more favorable than those that are available to the general public. In fact, some credit card or insurance products may be available only through prescreened offers.

If you do request to opt out, your request will be processed within five days, but it may take up to 60 days before you stop receiving prescreened offers. You can use the same toll-free telephone number or the website to opt back in.

And while we're at it, if you also want to remove your name and phone number from any tele-marketing lists, sign yourself up for the federal government's National Do Not Call Registry. According to the FTC, it is a free, easy way to reduce the telemarketing calls you get at home.

To register your phone number or to get information about the registry, visit donotcall.gov, or call 1-888-382-1222 from the phone number you want to register. You will get fewer telemarketing calls within 31 days of registering your number. Telephone numbers on the registry will only be removed when they are disconnected and reassigned, or when you choose to remove a number from the registry.

Monitor Credit Activity

Many companies these days offer some type of credit monitoring service that will alert you in case of any new credit activity. These services are a great first recourse to discovering any outside attempts at identity theft or fraud.

When you sign up for credit monitoring services, you'll be notified by phone, e-mail, text, push notification—whatever you prefer—when credit activity takes place.

Hard inquiries for new credit applications generally raise the biggest flags, since these imply that new credit has been requested. If you didn't make the request, then you should investigate the origin of the inquiry and the creditor.

For credit monitoring, I've used Lifelock (lifelock. com) for years. The company charges a monthly fee to alert consumers by e-mail or phone whenever a new credit application is detected.

Credit Sesame's monitoring service also offers an extensive geolocating social security activity tracker, which can alert you as to the area where your SSN has been used for credit applications.

The three CRAs also offer monitoring, but I think that the third-party service providers do it comprehensively and with better data and technology.

In recent identity theft cases, thieves targeted the valid social security numbers of toddlers and newborn babies in for credit card and loan applications.

All the more reason to be vigilant about how and to whom you disclose you and your family's social security numbers.

Any sensitive paper documentation leaving your household should always be crosscut shredded and disposed of properly.

If You Have Little or No Credit History

Perhaps you are just starting out and have no credit to your name. Or, perhaps you have just always been of a cash mind-set, so you've never wanted credit cards.

If you're finding it difficult to get a credit reporting trail established, then the first step could be to obtain a secured credit card.

You can research secured credit cards online at Credit Karma or Credit Sesame, which offer many options for consumers interested in establishing or building credit using these tools.

A Word on Chexsystems

You may have never heard of ChexSystems, but it's essentially the reporting system used by banks and financial institutions to determine your banking reputation and history.

Financial institutions lose billions of dollars every year because of check fraud and abuse, which is why 80 percent of U.S. banks and credit unions belong to the ChexSystems network.

If you've repeatedly bounced checks, written fraudulent checks, set up online/outgoing payments without sufficient funds and neglected or failed to pay on negative bank balances and even had your account closed as a result of your activities, then your data is likely on a ChexSystems report.

If you've consistently abused your banking privileges in this way, then you may be rejected the next time you attempt to open a new checking or savings account with a bank on account of your ChexSystems history.

Don't freak out because of the ghosts of two bad checks. Banks are looking for repeat offenders who make a practice out of writing bounced checks, overdrawing their accounts, or leaving accounts unpaid with negative balances, charges, and fees.

More importantly, banks simply want to avoid check fraud and money laundering. Red flags include when a person supplies inaccurate identifying information to open accounts.

For example, attempts at opening more than one account in less than a three-month period hints at "check kiting," where people take advantage of the float time of available funds to create fraudulent balances. A person may write a check to himself from one account to another, knowing fully well that the check will bounce. But this person plays the float during the time between the deposit of the check and the bouncing of the check, similar to how he writes bad checks in hopes that they will clear by payday.

You should know that ChexSystems itself does not have the authority to approve or deny any bank account applications; it merely reports your history to financial institutions. So ChexSystems is only the messenger, and you can't shoot the messenger.

ChexSystems also offers a risk management solution to financial institutions called QualiFile. QualiFile uses more comprehensive information than just past bank account history to predict the likelihood that a consumer will be a good account manager into the future, and in this way, mimics FICO credit scoring models.

This includes data from consumer credit reports, plus third-party entities that provide consumer financial and nonfinancial data such as check printing history, retail scans of checks, credit report data, and payday loan histories. All of these data combine to create a ChexSystems Consumer Score that financial institutions may use to predict future banking behavior.

Bank Account Alternatives

So what happens if you are denied a bank account? The reason may not be fraud-related. There are options to getting you back on track, and hope is not lost.

Roughly 15 percent of bank account applicants denied regular accounts are instead offered 'second chance' checking accounts or prepaid cards.

Banks may require money management classes with these second chance accounts, and new account holders must not incur overdrafts or write any bounced checks during a probationary period.

For example, as of this writing PNC Bank's Foundations checking program offers a 90-minute money management course which must be completed before the bank will offer a debit card, albeit with limited withdrawal privileges. If the account is managed well, then the customer can obtain a standard checking account.

If you're shopping around for prepaid card options, just beware of the fees involved. As of this writing, Chase's Liquid Prepaid Card, which comes with a $4.95 fee and allows customers to deposit checks at branches and ATMs for free, could be a cheaper alternative to some second chance checking accounts.

If you're curious about your personal Chex-Systems report, you can obtain one by going to consumerdebit.com or writing to:

Chex Systems Inc.
7805 Hudson Road, Suite 100
Woodbury, MN 55125

ChexSystems is considered a credit bureau and is monitored by the FCRA, so consumers are entitled to free annual reports. If you're curious as to what a ChexSystems report looks like, you can also find a sample consumer report from the site.

Your Turn

It's now your turn to implement the strategies discussed in this book.

Take a look at which credit rules apply to you and set-up an attack plan for improving your credit standing. Remember that credit is scored according to a formula, and if you play by that formula, then you can tip the scale in your favor.

If you get lost along the way, revisit Chapter 4 for the factors that make up a credit score, one by one.

Just because you can't pay off your credit debt all at once, you can pay it off according to scoring tiers.

Paying your bills on time will certainly help your score, too. But on-time payments and low debt balances hose are only two factors. The other components (not applying for new credit, building a credit history, and mixing up the types of your credit) play a part, too.

Remember, while there are some quick ways to boost your score, keeping an excellent score requires understanding and discipline.

If you'd like to share your stories with me, please drop me a line at tccn@thescri.be. I'd love to hear how these strategies helped you improve your credit, your greatest financial asset.

Subscribe to The Credit Cleanup Newsletter
for updates!
Visit tccbonline.com/newsletter

Follow the author:
Facebook.com/shindychenwrites
Twitter: @shindychen

Other personal finance books by Shindy Chen:
The Credit Cleanup Book

About the Author

Shindy Chen is a bestselling Amazon lifestyle and financial author. She contributes to The Huffington Post and speaks on innovations in consumer lending and millennial money matters, She has also been featured as a credit and personal finance expert on Cheddar TV, and in Girlboss, Forbes, and Marie Claire. Shindy is the founder of Scribe, a content consultancy and independent publishing house.

During her 7-year lending career, Shindy funded over $100 million in consumer loans, and served as a V.P. in retail loan origination at Wachovia Bank, now Wells Fargo. She then worked in financial broadcast news at CNBC in the U.S. and at Bloomberg TV in London. Recently, Shindy was the content manager at robo-advisor Betterment.

In 2014 she wrote, "The Credit Cleanup Book: Improving Your Credit Score, Your Greatest Financial Asset" (Praeger). "Credit Score Hacks" is her follow-up to that book.